Maggie
BY MY SIDE

Maggie
BY MY SIDE
≈ ≈
by Beverly Butler

DODD, MEAD & COMPANY

New York

PICTURE CREDITS

Lawrence Abrams, 2, 22, 44, 48, 53, 64, 74, 77, 80, 82, 90, 93; *The Milwaukee Journal,* 12 (left); Milwaukee Public Library, 17; *The Milwaukee Sentinel,* 12 (right); Pilot Dogs, Inc., 25, 26, 33, 57, 67, 72; Sterling Steffensen, 9.

1 2 3 4 5 6 7 8 9 10

Library of Congress Cataloging-in-Publication Data

Butler, Beverly.
  Maggie by my side.

  Summary: The author describes her experiences at Pilot Dogs, a facility in Ohio where she trained with a guide dog.
  1. Guide dogs—Training—Juvenile literature.
[1. Guide dogs.   2. Blind.   3. Physically handicapped]
I. Title.
HV1780.S4B87   1987   362.4'183   86-32883
ISBN 0-396-08862-7

For Jay
and all the other dedicated people
in guide dog work
who never doubt it's worth it

One

UNA, my golden retriever guide dog, lifted her head from where she lay dozing beside my desk. I felt her shift against my foot and knew from the jingle of the tags on her collar that she was looking toward the door.

The creative writing class I was teaching that week at the Rhinelander School of Arts, a summer workshop for artists and writers, didn't interest her much, but a stir in the halls close to the noon hour most certainly did.

"Una thinks it's lunchtime," I told the class, and touched the raised dots on my Braille watch to check. "She's right. Time to call it quits for today."

The class chuckled in agreement. Papers rustled, chairs scraped, and hungry would-be writers started for the door.

Nearly everyone stopped on the way out to give Una a pat or a word of praise. She stood up, waving her plume of a tail in approval, accepting the attention as her due. She was beautiful and she was special, and she knew it.

When I picked up the handle on her harness, she was ready to go. We joined the stream of people in the corridor and moved smoothly down the length of one hall and then another. A third turn brought us past the crowded commons already noisy with early lunchers, and on into the foyer to the school's front door, where my husband, Ted, would be arriving soon to drive us home.

I could tell by the way Una's tail kept brushing lightly across the back of my leg that she was pleased with herself.

I was pleased, too. I bent and rubbed her silky ears. "Good girl, Una."

Una,
a golden retriever

Yesterday, the first day of class, Ted had helped us find the room assigned to me, and he had come there afterward to guide us back along the new route. Today Una and I had found the way ourselves.

It wasn't a new experience, of course, for either of us. We had been together over six years now, traveling in every sort of circumstance from walking a country road to a neighbor's home to boarding a plane to keep a speaking date in a distant city. But for me, the feel of independence, no matter how modest the scale, never grows dull.

The day had nothing else particularly outstanding to offer. It was Tuesday, July 23, 1985—just another summer day in northern Wisconsin. Which is why it stands out particularly in my memory.

At home again, Una and I strolled down to the woods at the end of our yard in the late afternoon. I sat in a lawn chair, listening to the birds, while she rambled free under the nearby trees, trampling happily through the underbrush and snuffling at intriguing scents. That evening she ate a hearty supper as usual, and as usual begged a rawhide treat from Ted at bedtime. Shortly after, she was contentedly curled in her usual place beside the bed.

But she wasn't at my bedside in the morning. She wasn't even in the bedroom.

Ted found her in the laundry room beyond the kitchen, lying beside her water pail. The pail, which I had filled last night when I fed her, was more than half empty and her stomach was swollen as though she had swallowed a watermelon whole.

Her tail flopped up and down in an attempt to wag when I knelt beside her, but she didn't want to stand, much less touch her morning Milk-Bone.

"It's okay," I told her. "It's going to be all right."

How I hoped that was the truth as I dialed the number of the veterinary clinic to tell them my dog needed emergency attention.

I had to say good-bye to her there on the laundry floor. Ted bundled her up in his arms, big sixty-eight-pound dog that she was, and carried her out to the car, but I couldn't go along. There was my School of Arts class waiting to be taught.

I went back to the phone to arrange for someone from the school to give me a ride. Not until class was over at noon would I have a chance to hear what had gone wrong.

That was an endless morning. Over and over again as the class assembled by ones and twos, I answered the questions, "Where's Una?" "Isn't your dog here today?" Over and over again during the class period I caught myself about to drop my hand to fondle her ears or stroke her head. For six years she had been almost constantly at my left side when we weren't at home. It felt like being only half-dressed in public to sit there without her.

Noon came at last. The classroom emptied quickly, then the halls. The sounds of voices and feet faded away.

This day I wasn't free to get up from my desk and follow. I sat where I was and waited.

At last there were footsteps again in the hall. They paused in the doorway, and Ted cleared his throat. He made no other sound for a long moment.

I knew at once that when he did speak, I wouldn't want to hear what he had to say.

"They couldn't save her," he said finally. "Dr. Foster took her into surgery right away, but she was too far gone. She was full of cancer, and she was hemorrhaging badly inside. That's why she drank all the water—to make up for loss of blood."

Cancer? That didn't seem possible. My second guide dog, Heidi, had died of cancer, and it had been a lingering, painful illness that had robbed her by stages of weight, strength, and appetite. Una had shown no sign of any such distress.

Later, I learned from Dr. Race Foster of

the Rhinelander Veterinary Medical Center that Una's cancer was a type that spreads swiftly and without pain that might betray its presence. Una couldn't have had it more than a month, and very probably the worst discomfort she suffered was giddiness and thirst from her internal bleeding in the final hours. In that respect, at least, the killer had been merciful.

That knowledge still lay in the future, though. Nor would knowing have helped much right then. I wasn't ready yet to be grateful for small favors.

My dog was dead. Suddenly, incredibly gone. Forever. Until I got used to that, nothing else mattered.

How much I had lost began to sink in as I left the building, holding to Ted's arm instead of Una's harness. I stumbled on the walk outside, not certain where the curb was and not sure Ted would remember to warn me in time. With Una, I wouldn't have worried. Curb warnings were a routine part of her job.

How was I going to get through the remaining two days of the School of Arts without her?

The next morning I packed a folding cane

---

in my briefcase along with my Braille notes for class, although cane travel is a skill I've never truly mastered. When noon came and scores of lunch-bound people poured into the halls, my courage deserted me. What if I tripped up someone out there, swinging my cane to and fro? Or drifted too far to the left or right and blundered into a half-open door or knocked over one of the display tables?

So, again, I sat where I was and waited for Ted to come and fetch me.

Sit and wait. How many hours of my life had I spent with nothing to do but sit and wait?

I was fourteen when I lost my sight to glaucoma, a condition that destroys the optic nerve by a slow buildup of pressure inside the eye. My life before that had been fairly active. I biked to the homes of friends, to the library, rode the buses to programs at the museum, joined the clubs I liked best at school, went swimming in summer, skating in winter, and in every season roamed the woods and parkways near my home as I pleased.

Blindness put an end to all that. Where I went and when I went and how long I stayed became a question of whether there was someone available and willing to take me. If my plans didn't fit into those of another person, I didn't go. Not even for a walk around the block. There was nowhere I could go alone beyond the familiar boundaries of my own yard.

A schoolmate neighbor took me to school and home every day. At school, various classmates were assigned to walk me from one class to the next. If anyone had business elsewhere to attend to first, I sat and waited, sometimes so long that I began to be afraid I'd been forgotten altogether.

Then, the summer before my senior year of high school, I came home from a month's training at the Pathfinder school in Detroit with my first guide dog, Sister, a Doberman pinscher. That fall I traveled to and from school on my own, to and from my classes by myself, took satisfying walks alone when I felt like it, made dates to meet friends without worrying how I'd get there. Because of Sister, my world belonged to me again on my terms.

Sister saw me on through college and the budding of my writing career. After she died of leukemia in her eleventh year, there was Heidi, a German shepherd, who shared my term at graduate school and my first years of teaching. Another German shepherd, Chip, was with me when I met and married Ted.

Lastly, there was Una.

No, not last. Most recently.

I shifted in my chair, freshly aware of the vacant space beside me. It hurt to think of any dog but Una there, as once it had hurt to imagine any but Chip, or Heidi, or Sister by my side.

But if dogs have one great failing, it is that

Sister, a Doberman pinscher   *Heidi, a German shepherd*

Chip,
a German
shepherd

they live far shorter lives than the humans who love and need them. There would have to be another dog—one day. Not to help me forget Una, but because I could never forget what she and those before her had meant to me.

Footsteps were approaching in the hall. I stood up and pushed the chair under the desk.

Next week perhaps, or as soon as I could bear the thought better, I would begin to make plans for training with a new dog.

Two

THERE is no record of when a blind person first tied a rope around a willing dog's neck and followed where the dog led, thus greatly improving the chances of keeping to the path and out of the ditch. Pictures and writings that have come down to us through the ages suggest the practice was already commonplace in ancient times.

This is hardly surprising. The desire to please is a strong part of a dog's nature. Once a dog understands what its master wants, it will do almost anything asked of it for the sake of an approving pat or a word of praise. And no one who has ever hurtled down a street behind an enthusiastic dog at the other end of the leash can doubt that it is also in dog nature to lead.

What is surprising is that tens of centuries went by before anyone thought seriously of giving dogs special training to do guide work.

The first real training school was established in Germany during World War I to serve blinded German soldiers. Mrs. Dorothy Harrison Eustace, a wealthy American dog breeder living in Europe after the war, was so impressed by the German achievement that she wrote an article about it for the *Saturday Evening Post* entitled "The Seeing Eye."

Almost immediately, she was flooded with mail from blind people in the United States wanting her to train guide dogs for them. She finally invited a college student, Morris Frank, to travel to Fortunate Fields, her European estate, to be trained with one of her prize German shepherds. The change from Morris who needed to be taken everywhere he went to Morris and his new dog, Buddy, striding off on their own to find the barbershop in town was dramatic. In 1929, Mrs. Eustace sent money, dogs, and a trainer to the United States to found the Seeing Eye school in New Jersey.

World War II brought a need for more such schools. There were eleven to choose from in the United States when I began to consider where to apply after losing Una.

Through the years other schools have appeared and disappeared. Pathfinder, where I received my first dog, Sister, came to the end of its existence with the death of its owner-founder. The school that trained my second dog, Heidi, AA of Lake Ripley, Wisconsin, eventually failed for lack of sufficient finances.

None of the guide dog schools receives any government funding. They rely on private donations and public support to keep going. The cost of training a dog and a blind person to work together is in the neighborhood of $3,200. None of the schools ask the blind student to pay more than $150 of this, and some ask no payment at all.

For many people who don't know better, any guide dog is a Seeing Eye dog. However, that is about the same as insisting that every car on the road is a Ford. Each guide dog school has its own name and its own personality.

I decided to start by writing for information to four or five on the list before making up my mind where to apply. The first chilly warnings of winter were already creeping into the Northwoods country as I addressed the letters. Schools in California—Guide Dogs for the Blind, San Rafael, and International Guiding Eyes, Sylmar—sounded tempting. There was also the appeal of renewing old friendships and associations at Guiding Eyes for the Blind, Yorktown Heights, New York, where I had trained with Una.

What I was really wishing for, though, if it could possibly be arranged, was that my next dog would be a German shepherd. Most dog people, I've noticed, have one breed or type of mixture that speaks to them more loudly than the rest. For me it's the shepherd.

Una was as beautiful, gentle, and sweet-tempered a dog as I have ever known. What caused us problems now and then was that she was also the most resolutely low-keyed. Her code was: "A golden retriever cannot be hurried." Not by a truck roaring down on us as we

crossed the street. Not by a cloudburst catching us a block from home and shelter. Not by my urging that at this rate we were sure to miss the bus.

It's true that no truck ever did hit us. Our bus never did go without us. And we probably would have been no less soaked had we run through the rain instead of sauntered. Still, as she and I ambled sedately along, no matter what, I couldn't help a wistful thought sometimes of the brisk pace of my shepherds, who believed that if getting there was half the fun, the other half was getting there first.

Besides that, there was the nagging question in my mind: if Una had been less languid by nature, might I have spotted some hint of her illness earlier? Perhaps early enough to have saved her?

As replies to my letters began to arrive, however, each school in turn reminded me that, although my preference for a particular breed would be noted, the trainer makes the final decision as to which dog a student will receive.

There is good reason for this, of course.

"For me, it's the shepherd."

———

No one knows the traits of the individual dogs—fast walkers or slow, hard pullers or easy, superfriendly or aloof, docile or in need of no-nonsense handling—better than the trainer, who has been working with them daily for three to four months. The trainer studies the new students, too, sometimes for two or three days, walking with them, talking to them, judging how sure they are on their feet, what their normal pace is, whether they are likely to be firm or mild in giving a dog corrections. Then, putting these observations together, the trainer tries to make the best matches possible between dogs and people.

Unfortunately, the number of German shepherds selected for training as guide dogs has dwindled considerably. Guiding Eyes, I learned, had graduated only two in the last year. Labrador retrievers and goldens account for a large portion of dogs used today, plus boxers, Doberman pinschers, Vizslas, and a sprinkling of other breeds and crossbreeds.

For one thing, many people who need a dog to get them to and from work also need one that is willing to lie quietly during the long hours in between. A placid golden retriever is

BREEDS OF DOGS
USED AS GUIDE DOGS

*German
shepherd*

Boxer

Labrador retriever

Vizsla

Doberman pinscher

happier with that sort of schedule than an en-
ergy-packed shepherd.

Another reason is that truly good German

shepherds have come to be in short supply in this country. Over the years, too many breeders have concentrated on producing a fashionably streamlined specimen for the show-ring without much regard for intelligence or temperament or stamina. This has created strains of high-strung, unstable, and structurally weak dogs that are unsuited for guide work.

One school, Fidelco, in Connecticut, does use only German shepherds. These are dogs bred especially from working—not show—dogs imported from Germany. Because Fidelco trainers and dogs go to the homes of the students to train instead of the students boarding at a school, the service is restricted to people in the Connecticut-New York area. Living in Wisconsin, I was too far away to qualify.

Another disappointment was that each of the other schools advised me to plan on a stay of 23 to 28 days before I could bring my new dog home. When I trained with Heidi and again with Chip, two weeks had been considered a long enough refresher course for students who were already experienced in using a guide dog.

There was no returning to Heidi's school. It wasn't there any more. But Pilot Dogs where

I received Chip was still where it had always been, in Columbus, Ohio.

I flipped through my address book, wondering why I had stopped my letter writing short of the P's. I'd heard that Pilot had undergone some changes since I was there—could it really be nineteen years ago?—but perhaps not everything was different.

Suddenly I didn't want to wait for a letter to travel to Ohio and a reply to come back. I picked up the phone and punched in the number for information.

Within five minutes, I was speaking to John Gray in Pilot Dogs' office. To my surprise, he remembered me and that we both had once lived in Milwaukee.

"What can we do for you?" he asked. I told him, a little apologetically because by now even I was beginning to suspect my hopes were utterly unreasonable.

"No problem," John said.

"No problem about what?" I was so braced for a refusal, I wasn't sure I had heard him right.

"About anything. If we trained you once, it had to be a good enough job so that we can train you again in two weeks."

"With a shepherd?" I still wasn't quite believing my ears.

"If you've had a shepherd before and want one again, we'll train you with a shepherd. We feel you'll both start out happier that way." He paused while the rain splashing down outside my window turned to music. "That is, if we can find a shepherd we can talk into going to Wisconsin."

THE weeks following that phone call were full of plans, preparations, and waiting.

I sorted through my closet, selecting the sturdiest and most comfortable of my walking shoes, the most respectable yet durable of my shirts and pants. Training, as I well knew, takes place mostly out of doors and on foot in all kinds of weather.

I bought a pack of rawhide sticks and a

canvas tug-of-war toy to help make friends with the new dog.

Then there were forms to fill out describing our home, our way of life, and the conditions under which the new dog would be living and working.

There was a medical questionnaire to be answered and signed by my doctor after she put me through a physical exam.

If this had been my first application to Pilot Dogs, there would also have been letters to be signed by organizations and people who knew me, stating that I did need a dog, would use a dog, could afford to feed one, and that, above all, I could be trusted to care for and never abuse one. The schools reserve the right to take back a dog that is mistreated or misused.

At last the call came from John Gray: "We have a beautiful German shepherd ready for you. Is the seventh of October too soon for you to be here?"

"No, that's fine," I said eagerly, without even pausing to calculate that October 7 was less than a week and a half away. The only question I could think of was: "What's the dog's name?"

"Maggie," John said.

Maggie. I rolled the name over in my mind as I hung up the receiver. Yes, I liked it.

For one thing, it wasn't a name that already belonged to any of the other members of our household: Jasper and Charlie, the cats, and Mike, our black Labrador, who keeps Ted company nearly everywhere he goes. Neither was Maggie the name of a friend or relative or neighbor. In the days when Heidi was my guide it seemed as if at least one child in every block was named Heidi, and her mother was out calling her as we went by.

Worse were the troubles I met on enrolling at a Catholic college, Mount Mary in Milwaukee, with a dog named Sister. Practically all my teachers were nuns, School Sisters of Notre Dame, and were properly addressed as "Sister," too. The day I told my dog firmly, "Sister, sit," and my logic professor turned from adjusting the window to inquire rather coldly, "I beg your pardon?"—that day I changed my dog's name to Sissy.

Sister; Heidi; Chip; Una—and now Maggie. Suddenly my excitement turned to dismay. How could I welcome a new dog into my life so soon? I wasn't used to missing Una yet.

Nevertheless, the tickets arrived from Pilot Dogs within a few days, and on a crisp fall morning I boarded the plane for Columbus. Hours later, I deplaned into a summer-warm afternoon, feeling as nervous as if I were about to be married to a stranger.

"Hello, Beverly? I'm Jay, from Pilot Dogs," a pleasant voice with a decided Ohio flavor greeted me, and a big hand shook mine.

Jay was to be my trainer for the next two weeks, I learned on the drive from the airport to the school. I was coming in at the midpoint of a class that had been underway for two weeks

Pilot Dogs, Inc., Columbus, Ohio

already. With me and two other newcomers expected today, the class would number seven.

I wanted to ask about Maggie. What was she like? But what could he tell me that I wouldn't be discovering for myself in a very short while? Besides, I knew from past experience that trainers, for some reason, are cautious about giving out too much information about a dog until they are fairly certain that the dog and student really are going to make it as a working team.

I knew, too, that it was too late in the day to hope to meet Maggie before tomorrow. We arrived at the school close to the supper hour. Jay had time only to show me to my room, give me brief directions to the dining room, and introduce me to my roommate, Chris, who was halfway through her training with an amiable black Lab called Bo.

I unpacked after supper, and then spent part of the evening getting reacquainted with the building, which had grown and changed since my training days here with Chip.

A whole new wing of students' quarters had been added. More surprising, the dayroom, where everyone gathers to relax between training walks, was almost double the size I remembered. A color TV, a stereo radio phonograph, cupboards of games and shelves of Braille books, a pay phone booth, a table holding two type-writers and a Braille writer with paper to use in them, a piano and an electric organ were all fitted in without crowding among an ample number of upholstered armchairs.

The old snack bar had become a nook at one side of the dayroom. It still was a restaurant-type booth, though, where dogs could get used to lying out of the way under the bench while their owners enjoyed a soft drink from the vending machine.

The tour was interesting, but I was glad when Chris announced to the others in the dayroom that she thought she would turn in early. That was in my mind, too. The sooner I could call this a day, the sooner tomorrow would be here—and Maggie.

I heard Chris snap on the light as I followed her into our room. "Can you see light?" I asked.

I have no vision whatever, but the term "blind" can mean any sort of poor vision from none to sight enough to read print with a magnifying lens.

_____

"I see some light," Chris said. She laughed. "But Jay told us to put the light on for our dogs because it makes them more comfortable."

That was a new rule to me, but not exactly a surprise. More than once at home I'd been reminded to turn on the lights by the restless way the animals were behaving.

Chris moved to the window and clattered the metal blinds shut. "Another thing they told us was to remember to close these when the light's on. Because other people can see in here even if we can't see out."

When we were both settled in our beds and the light was off again, we went on talking for a while. Chris was from Cedar Rapids, Iowa, she told me, where she had lived alone in her own apartment. Bo was her second dog. Her first dog had taken ill this past year. After repeated treatment and soaring veterinary bills, she had been declared unfit for further guide dog work. Chris had finally accepted a friend's offer to take the dog and give her a good home for the remainder of her life.

"What else could I do?" Chris asked. "I need a dog, a working dog, and I can't afford to keep two."

So she had parted with her aging dog one Sunday morning, and had taken the plane for Pilot Dogs in the afternoon.

"When I got here, I just lay down on the bed and cried. I cried and cried. I couldn't stop. Then Jay came in and told me if I didn't quit, he wouldn't give me another dog. He wasn't going to have me upsetting a new dog that way."

She paused and drew a breath. "So I managed to stop. And Bo and I are doing real well. And I try not to think about anything else."

She had managed superbly, I thought, for my impression of her at supper was of a bubbly, friendly young woman without a care in the world.

I lay awake a long time after Chris drifted off to sleep and Bo, on his tie-down chain beside her bed, began softly snoring. Pilot Dogs is located close to downtown Columbus. Sounds of traffic, squealing tires, car horns poured in through the window. A party was going on across the street, complete with bursts of laughter, loud music, and an endlessly yapping small dog. At home at this hour there would be nothing to hear but the wind in the trees or possibly a solitary car passing along our road.

———

I kept thinking of Chris's story. Perhaps I was lucky, after all. Una was gone totally and forever. I wouldn't be torn by thoughts of her waiting for me somewhere, wondering why I'd left her, when I met Maggie tomorrow.

Maggie and I would be starting fresh.

Four

"BEVERLY, do you want to get your harness and meet me out at the gate?"

It was a question that could have only one answer. Jay knew I had been sitting in the day-room since breakfast, waiting for just that invitation.

Chris and Bo were already back from their morning walk. As I hurried into our room, I could hear her in the courtyard outside our window, urging Bo to make the most of his chance to use the dog run before they came in.

The harness Jay had given me last night lay on top of the wardrobe where I had put it for safekeeping. I lifted it down, appreciating the stiff newness of the leather.

Each of the guide dog schools uses a harness somewhat different in detail from those of the others, but the basic design is the same. There are two broad straps, one across the chest and one that fits over the back to fasten underneath with a buckle. Attached to these is the handle, shaped like a squared U. The base of the U is a leather-covered handgrip. On the Pilot Dog harness, the shafts are sheathed in bright orange plastic to make the harness more visible on busy streets.

The earliest guide dog harnesses had a flexible strap instead of a handle. It was soon discovered, however, that a rigid handle is far easier to follow. The vibrations that travel up those shafts carry an astonishing amount of information about the dog's slightest movements, even to the brief stretch of the neck to steal a forbidden sniff at something.

This is a telegraph that sends messages in both directions. The dogs are quick to pick up on little signals they receive from the human end of the handle.

Once when I was doing my best to behave civilly to a person I privately did not like, I dropped my hand to Chip at my side and was startled to find the hair bristling along her spine. My act might be fooling our visitor, but Chip knew how I really felt and saw no reason to hide it.

At college it was a standing joke among my friends that they could tell if I were well prepared or not at exam time by watching Sister. If she lay tense and nervous at my feet, it was bad news. If she rested her head on her paws and went to sleep, all was well. My friends—and Sister—were usually right.

And now I was on my way down the hall with a brand-new harness hung over my arm, about to open a brand-new line of communication.

I pushed through the glass door into the courtyard and followed the paved walk along the building. A right turn at the building's end brought me out of cool shade into hot sunshine. The gate was close by here somewhere, but I wasn't quite sure where.

I halted, listening for Jay. What I heard was the scrape of toenails on the concrete to my left and a dog panting excitedly.

"Here she is," Jay said, putting the end of a leash into my hand. "This is Maggie. Take a few minutes to get acquainted. Then harness her up and we'll go for a walk."

"Maggie." I held my hand down toward her. "Hello, Maggie."

Unlike Una, who had flung herself joyously into my arms at the first words I spoke to her, Maggie sniffed me politely but with no great interest.

That was disappointing, but I should have been prepared. Both Heidi and Chip, my other shepherds, had been cool at the start, too—not unfriendly but not particularly thrilled to meet me, either. Their love wasn't a free handout; it had to be won. But it was well worth the winning.

Maggie stood quietly while I ran my hands over her to get an idea of what she was like. All I knew of her so far was that she was about eighteen months old and weighed in the neighborhood of fifty-eight pounds. That made her about ten pounds lighter than Una.

She was also shorter than Una from front to back, I discovered. In height, however, they were about the same. One of the requirements for guide dog work is that the dog measure between twenty-three and twenty-five inches high at the shoulder. A larger dog becomes a problem fitting into cars or out of the way under restaurant tables or theater seats. A smaller dog is an awkward height to walk beside.

Maggie's tail hung in a graceful curve that turned up at the tip, suggesting that she wasn't unhappy even though she wasn't ready yet to wag it for me. She bobbed her head away when I touched her alertly pointed ears, but when I held up the harness, she swung back and thrust her head through the opening. If we were going somewhere, she was ready.

"Okay, let's go," Jay said as I straightened up from fastening the buckle. "Turn right at the sidewalk. Go to the first down curb and stop."

He clanked the heavy wire mesh gate open for us. "Maggie, forward," I said, and we moved out.

———

I didn't know just how far the gate was from the sidewalk, so after a few steps, I said, "Maggie, right."

Maggie led me briskly onward half a dozen steps more, showing no sign she had heard. Then, without breaking stride, she turned right and trotted purposefully on down the sidewalk.

We came to a smart stop at the edge of a wall of noise. Cars were whizzing by at what sounded like only inches from our noses. I slid my right foot forward to locate the curb, which I knew would be there.

"Good girl, Maggie," I praised, putting a lot of feeling into it.

Maggie turned her head, but not to look at me. She wanted her praise from Jay, who came up beside us.

Jay ignored her. She was my dog now, and she had to begin learning that I was the master.

"You're facing Town Street," Jay told me. "Grub is on your left. This corner is light-controlled."

We stood there listening to the rush of traffic. It was coming from every direction at

Harnessing up

———

once without any kind of pattern to it. Or so it sounded to my ears, used to the quiet of woodland roads where an approaching car can be heard a quarter mile away and as many as three cars approaching at once is a minor happening.

He's not going to tell me to decide when it's safe to cross, I reassured myself. But I knew he was. If not today, then tomorrow or the next day.

In theory, crossing at a light-controlled corner is fairly simple. If the flow of traffic is passing in front of you, you wait at the curb and listen for the flow to change. When the traffic alongside you starts up, you go, too, in the same direction. Simple, unless the truck in the farther lane is gunning its engine with a roar that masks every other sound until it's too late to cross, or a car turning right on red zooms into your path as you step off the curb.

Deciding when it is safe to cross is the master's responsibility. Dogs don't read traffic lights. To the best of my knowledge, dogs don't even look at them. The dog's job is to get the team safely to the opposite curb after the master gives the command to go ahead.

Jay took pity on me this time. "Okay, forward. When you get to the other side, keep on straight to the next corner."

I drew a short breath and said more firmly than I felt, "Maggie, forward."

We plunged into the heart of the uproar without a quiver on Maggie's part. She marched me through the ranks of snarling engines as calmly as if they were so many chirping crickets, and paused at the up curb to let me know we had arrived.

We crossed several more streets on that walk, some governed by stop-lights, some by stop signs, and some—generally the quieter ones, thank goodness—by nothing at all. The only way to tell the difference was to listen to the way the traffic stopped and started.

By the time our route brought us back to the Pilot Dog gate, I was beginning to think I just might be able to handle busy crossings by myself someday in the far-off future. I didn't have a doubt in the world about Maggie's ability to do it.

"Nice job for a first walk," Jay said, rattling the gate shut behind us. "Take her harness off and give her some time in the run. She can have water today, but don't feed her supper. She's

going to be pretty tensed up and nervous, so she probably wouldn't keep it down."

Maggie watched him walk away from us. I urged her into the run, a concrete area surrounded by an elbow-high railing where students can lean while they wait for their dogs to relieve themselves, but she merely stood there, staring in the direction Jay had gone and whining softly.

For the past four months since her family had donated her to be a Pilot Dog, Jay had been the one dependable human in her life. He had come to the kennel daily to train and praise and play with her. Now he seemed suddenly to be deserting her, handing her over to a stranger, and everything she'd grown used to was being changed again.

Little wonder if her stomach should be upset by the end of this day.

In shopping mall

———

Five

AT lunch that noon there were seven students gathered at the long dining table—and seven dogs underneath it: four Labs, a Doberman, a Vizsla, and Maggie.

There were no dog fights, surprisingly, but the table talk was punctuated by remarks from Jay at the head of the table such as: "Pete, your dog's chewing the chair rung." "Julie, Chris, your dogs are together playing footsies. Get them back where they belong and make them stay." "Good correction, Sarah. Let her know you mean it when you say no." "Beverly, your dog is up again."

I lowered my grilled cheese sandwich to my plate and reached for Maggie. With one hand I gave a push to her rear, with the other a short jerk on her leash, and said, "Down."

She bobbed down, away, and up like a plastic duck in a bathtub. Now she was facing me from a little farther under the table, her legs braced against the pull of the leash.

We went through the same struggle twice more before I got her to lie down properly again beside my chair so I could return to my sandwich.

Three bites later, she was on her feet, peering over the edge of the table as if she had been called.

I don't know how many times we repeated our wrestling match to force her down, but I do know it never took me longer to finish a sandwich. Somewhere between our morning walk and the call to lunch, Maggie had changed from a well-behaved, willing dog to a stubborn, willful mule.

Our training walk that afternoon was no

better. Instead of crossing straight from curb to curb at the corner, she angled left to sniff a pile of leaves in the gutter. At the next corner she stopped about a foot short of the curb so that I had to fumble with my foot to find it. On the sidewalk, she shambled along at a maddening shuffle as if her battery were nearly dead.

"Stop!" Jay yelled suddenly from behind us.

I stopped instantly. A yell like that could mean any sort of disaster about to happen at the next step.

Jay sprinted up beside us. "No," he told Maggie sternly, at the same time taking the leash from me and giving it a sharp jerk. He struck a hollow clang from a pole in front of me. "No."

Maggie cringed. So did I when Jay showed me the metal sign jutting from the pole at just about eye level. It could have meant a nasty bruise if not an open cut if I hadn't stopped in time.

People who see a blind person give a correction like that sometime jump to the conclusion that the person is being wickedly cruel to

Maggie at a restaurant

———

the dog. What they fail to consider is that a dog whose attention strays or who is allowed to grow careless can cause its master real injury or even death. The most highly trained dog in the world is still a dog, after all, and not a fur-clad piece of electronics programmed never to make a mistake or have an off day.

"Let's go back a way and try it over," Jay said.

Maggie and I did an about-face and re-traced our steps for several yards. I confess to feeling a degree less confidence in my dog as we turned to approach the sign a second time. Maggie's pace was less casual, too, but she didn't hesitate. A pleased "Good" from Jay told me we had passed the hazard with room to spare.

I bent and patted Maggie. "Very good girl."

For the first time, she looked around at me as if I were actually there. I had the impression she was almost ready to wag her tail.

"She took you by that pole fine this morning," Jay said. "She's goofing off this afternoon, trying to see how much she can get away with. Tomorrow after breakfast, give her some obedience. Let her know who's boss."

So Maggie was testing me. Already. Somewhere in the course of every new dog-and-master combination's becoming a team, there comes a time when the dog decides to check out how many of the old rules still apply under the new management. Often this happens along about the second week of training, but sometimes not until weeks or even months after dog and master have gone home.

The fact that Maggie was trying to turn the situation to her advantage on the very first day suggested a dog who caught on fast. It also suggested I would have to keep on my toes in handling her or we would shortly be doing things her way instead of mine.

Therefore, bright and early the next morning, Maggie and I withdrew to a deserted end of the corridor outside our room and proceeded to do obedience. That is, I proceeded to give the commands—heel, sit, down, stay, come. Maggie proceeded to roll on her back, nip at my shoes, and chew on the leash. She uttered shrill puppy yelps of excitement each time I opened my mouth, plainly trying to tell me what fun we could have if we didn't get too serious.

It was hard not to laugh at her, and harder to ignore the invitation to play. I wanted her to start really liking me and being glad she was my dog.

But I couldn't forget a talk Jeffrey Locke, Director of Training at Guiding Eyes, had given the class when I was there with Una: "Your dog may be going down the road and see another dog on the left-hand side," he had said. "Thinking as all dogs do, it will be very much on your dog's mind to go toward that other one. If your dog loves you, it may or may not go past that other dog. If it respects you, it surely will."

So I stood Maggie on her feet, shortened my hold on the leash, and began again with a brisk, "Maggie, heel."

Just as she had been quick to take advantage of the shift from Jay's handling to mine, so she was quick to understand that now I did mean business. She straightened into heel position, and we went on through the drill, if not quite with show-ring polish, at least with a clear recognition of the difference between playtime and no-nonsense.

We did play afterward. I brought out the tug-of-war toy I had bought her, and for half an hour we played tug, catch, and keep-away with it in our room to her heart's content. But not until the morning's training walk was successfully behind us.

The obedience drill we did that morning and every morning from then on didn't magically change Maggie from a live dog to a windup robot, no longer interested in sniffing fireplugs or swerving to watch a squirrel climb a tree. It did impress on her that she should listen as carefully to commands from me as she ever did to Jay's. And it gave me a sense of being more in control.

Soon Jay began working us students in pairs, and I began to pay more attention to the street

Maggie quickly learned who was boss.

names he recited at each crossing on every walk. Little by little they shaped themselves into a map in my mind, so that when he directed us to cross Skidmore, turn right on Gift and go up to Rich, I had a fair idea we would be taking the bus to High Street for a walk among the crowds of shoppers there or to work our dogs on the escalators in a department store.

Learning to form mental maps is an important part of using a guide dog, too. If the blind person has no notion of where to find the bank—which way to turn at the corner, how many streets to cross, where to wait for the bus, how far to walk after getting off—merely telling the dog, "I want to go to the bank," isn't going to get them there. What the dog is trained to do is to turn right or left on command, to warn of stairs or steps by stopping at them, to cross in a direct line from one curb to another, and to lead the master safely around obstacles in the chosen path.

After our near miss with the signpost, I had some lingering doubts about Maggie on this last point until our third afternoon together. That afternoon Jay lined up all seven students at the gate and, without explanation, sent us off by two's to circle the block, one of us making all right turns, the other all left.

Maggie slowed to a stop halfway to the first corner. I urged her forward, but she wouldn't budge.

The thing to do in such a case is to put out a foot or a hand to discover if anything is blocking the way. I found a lawn chair sitting square in the middle of the walk, a broom laid across its arms.

"Good girl," I told Maggie. "It's okay. Go forward."

Maggie stood a moment as if puzzling it out. Then she edged me to the right, onto the lawn. A few steps more and we were back on the sidewalk, the chair behind us.

As we went on, Maggie swung wide to the right in one place, to the left in another, and at some places slowed to a cautious inching ahead. The whole block must have been turned into an obstacle course, I realized. Yet in four circuits of the block, two to the right, two to the left, I touched only one thing besides that chair. It was a two-by-four lying on the walk where it could trip someone. Maggie refused to step over it until I had explored it with my foot and told her it was all right to go forward.

At supper that evening Jay admitted that the training staff had set out everything they could think of to clutter the way. All of us, he added, students and dogs, had done well.

Under the table, Maggie laid her head on my foot and heaved a sigh as if that were old news. I knew exactly how she felt.

Six

JAY began working us in two's and three's, and having us take turns at giving the word when a street was safe to cross. My ears were growing sharper with practice. It was possible now to detect a pattern in the churning of traffic at most intersections, but there still were moments when I felt my go-ahead was a matter of one part conviction to two parts faith—faith that Jay knew that Pilot Dogs would frown on his letting any of us actually get killed.

We were coming up to one of these blankets of raw sound once when I heard footsteps approaching from behind us. Someone wearing cleats tramped past me, stepped off the curb without pause, and clicked boldly on toward the opposite curb.

Instantly, I said, "Maggie, forward." Pete and Julie gave their dogs the same command, and we were across that street in record time.

A second later, Jay was pacing along beside me. "Could it be you maybe cheated a little on that last one?"

"Maybe. A little," I admitted, rather pleased with myself.

Jay wasn't so pleased. "How did you know that guy wasn't some kook going to jump in front of a bus? How could you tell he wasn't drunk or stoned?"

He raised his voice for Pete and Julie to hear, too. "Don't trust sighted people to always know what they're doing just because they can see. They'll say anything to keep you moving. Like they'll tell you 'It's okay, the light's green' two seconds before it changes, and then you're out in the middle with everything coming at you."

Agreed. Following those cleats wasn't the smartest thing I'd ever done. But if they really had led us into the path of a bus, what would Maggie have done, I wondered.

The answer came the next day, sooner than I was ready for it. This time it was a fairly easy corner, where there were no confusing noises to mask the halting of traffic in front of us and its surge into motion on our right. Sarah, my partner this morning, gave her dog a "Forward," and I gave Maggie the same.

Once off the curb, both dogs hesitated briefly, then angled sharply left. "They're all right," Jay called. "Keep going. No, STOP!"

A second later he was between Sarah and me, taking charge of the rest of the crossing himself.

The problem, he explained when we were safely on the other side, was that a car waiting for the light was blocking the crosswalk. By leading us out in front of the car, the dogs might have swung us into the line of moving traffic. Instead, they started to do as they were trained: take us around behind.

All would have been well if the driver hadn't suddenly panicked at seeing us and, too late,

realized her car was where it shouldn't be. She quickly threw it into reverse to clear the way—and very nearly succeeded.

Jay aired his opinion of dumb women drivers for the next two blocks. Sarah and I found it hard to disagree with any of his points. Yet I felt more like celebrating than scolding after my pulse rate began to ease down to normal again. For Maggie had already stopped short of the car on her own before Jay's warning yell. She wasn't about to let us be heedlessly run over.

One triumph of that sort goes a long way, however. I wasn't regretful in the least when, instead of scheduling more walks for the afternoon, Jay loaded the whole class into the van after lunch and took us to visit the Pilot Dog kennel some two miles from the school.

The kennel can house up to 125 dogs at a time, one to a cage. From the din of barks that greeted us, it sounded as if the full count were there.

We made a hands-on inspection of an empty cage. It was large enough for all seven of us to

A guide dog can't read signs.

crowd inside while Jay stood at the door, describing the various features.

A four-foot-high wall separated it from the cages on either side to discourage fights between neighbors. From the top of the wall to the ceiling was steel mesh. A jump board about three feet off the floor provided a place for the dog to lie if the floor should be wet or messy or simply not a bed to the dog's liking. At the back of the cage a trapdoor opened into an outside run.

About half the dogs who become Pilot Dogs are donated by owners who want a good life for a pet they can no longer keep. The other half are raised in Pilot's own breeding program. The mother dogs live in the homes of volunteers and are brought to the kennel to be bred.

When the puppies are around six weeks old, they are placed in the homes of 4-H members or other volunteers for a year to grow up in a family atmosphere. The hard part comes when it's time to say good-bye at the end of that year, but it helps a little if the van that picks up the grown dog is carrying a box of fresh puppies wanting a home.

Donated or raised especially, every dog

Pups enrolled in Pilot Dogs' breeding program

goes into the isolation area for ten days on its arrival at the kennel. Here its physical condition is thoroughly checked and it is X-rayed for signs of hip dysplasia, a bone malformation that can lame or even cripple a young dog. All males are neutered and all females spayed.

———

On the day of our visit, there were forty-eight newly donated dogs in the isolation cages, waiting to start the four months of training that would change their lives and those of the persons whose guides they would become.

Would it be a happy change from the dogs' point of view? Our own dogs, locked in empty cages out of harm's way while we toured the kennel, greeted our return to them with what sounded like an overwhelming Yes. Even Maggie's tail was wagging as we headed back to the van.

That evening a team of three veterinarians met with us in the dayroom to administer the rabies shots our dogs needed before we took them home.

They were there, too, to answer any questions we had on how best to keep our dogs healthy and fit. A sick guide dog can not only cause its master a great deal of heartache; it can very nearly bring that master's life to a standstill—broken dates, missed days of school, lost time on the job.

Proper diet is important. Although some people still insist that dogs have cast-iron stomachs that can handle anything, a dog's digestive system is easily upset by the wrong food or even food different from what it usually gets. Sneaking treats to a guide dog without its master's permission is decidedly NOT the way to win its master's friendship.

I'll never forget a banquet I once attended. The woman seated opposite me kept remarking how unfair it was for us to be dining so well while that poor dog had to lie under the table, getting nothing. I explained to her that Chip had already been fed her supper; that she had a rather nervous stomach and I was careful about what she ate; that if she got the idea she could beg at table, she would become a nuisance that would make us both unwelcome in public eating places.

The woman was not impressed. She knew the truth was that I was simply a selfish pig without a thought for my devoted companion. "At least you can give your dog the bones left on your plate," she said at the end of the meal.

"Chicken bones? Those are the last things I'd give her," I said, shocked. "A splinter could pierce an intestine or her stomach wall and kill her."

"Really?" said the woman as she got up to

---

leave. "Well, she certainly enjoyed the ones I slipped to her."

For days afterward, I lived alert to Chip's every snuffle or sigh, watching for a sign of distress that might spell disaster. Fortunately, Chip escaped undamaged by the woman's "kindness."

Fortunately, too, for that woman, our paths didn't cross again; never have I felt so strong an urge to do murder.

"And now here's Maggie," one of the vets said, kneeling down beside her as if they were old friends. "She's a beautiful dog. How is she, a good worker?"

"They're all beautiful dogs and good workers," Jay said. "It's the students that give us the trouble."

That got him a cheerful volley of return insults, but he did have some justice on his side. Dogs didn't fake it at crossings; dogs didn't argue when he gave them advice; they didn't turn moody at the end of a trying day.

His job called for as great an ability to deal with people as to handle dogs. He and the other trainers were always ready with a serious answer to a serious question. They didn't hesitate to be firm when they had to, but mostly they kept the tone light and teasing, getting us to laugh at ourselves, our misgivings and mistakes, rather than brood on them.

To become a guide dog trainer, one must serve a two-year apprenticeship. It helps to have a college degree, especially in such courses as psychology, sociology, or zoology, but not all schools require it.

During the first year, apprentices work just with the dogs. They also spend a day blindfolded to get a feel of what it's like to be without sight.

In the second year they observe experienced trainers' classes and possibly help out. Finally, they take on a class of their own under supervision. Only then, if all goes well, do they qualify as full-fledged trainers.

"And that's when the real grief begins," Jay grumbled, still failing to recognize our superior merits.

I waited until my last day of training to ask: "Is it worth it?"

The question apparently wasn't new to him, for he didn't pause to think about the answer. "Yeah, it's worth it. When you see people come

Trainers spend time blindfolded.

in at the start of a class and they're timid and shuffling, all tensed up and nervous; and then when they leave they're striding along, their heads up and smiling—yeah, it's worth it."

Seven

ON a Friday morning as warm and summery as the day I had arrived, I was once more walking with Jay through the Columbus airport. The difference was that instead of saying hello, we were about to say good-bye, and instead of holding to Jay's arm for guidance, I was following Maggie as she trotted at my left side.

Two days earlier Maggie and I had passed our test walk. For this, each dog-and-student team was sent out alone to cover a route Jay outlined for us in advance. It involved crossing a number of light-controlled streets, boarding a bus for a brief ride, going into a specific store where we were to buy something—anything, it didn't matter what—and returning to the school in a similar fashion. One of the trainers, not Jay, trailed each team as a silent observer who would offer no comment or help unless we got into real difficulties. My purchase was a candy bar to be nibbled on and possibly shared with Maggie during the long hours we would be waiting in Chicago between planes.

For now our class was scattering across the country—to different parts of Ohio, to Florida and South Carolina, Wisconsin and Iowa, and on west to Washington. We were heading home with our new dogs.

Maggie lay down obediently at my feet on the plane, but I could feel her trembling as I fastened my seat belt. She didn't know what to expect of this odd sort of bus. It occurred to me while I soothed and patted her that I didn't know what to expect of her either. Not really. We were like a pair of newlyweds starting off

Selecting a toy for Maggie

on our honeymoon with a lot still to learn about each other in the months ahead.

Once we were airborne, Maggie relaxed. She weathered the trip like a seasoned traveler, greeted Ted politely when we landed in Rhinelander, and followed him to our car as if she'd always done it.

Introducing her into our household was something else again.

We began by having her meet our Labrador, Mike, outdoors. He was delighted to find a lovely young female in his front yard. Not so when she came indoors. The moment Maggie crossed the threshold, he shouldered and snarled her away from everything that was off limits to strange dogs in his house—which was, in fact, just about everything.

Maggie accepted this meekly enough that first night. But the next day, when Mike indicated in supreme macho style that he might relent a bit if she were as nice as she was pretty, it was too much. Maggie let him know with a snap of teeth and a rising of hair on her back

Mike, once he had accepted Maggie

exactly where she stood on female rights and where he could go if he didn't like it.

Mike, accustomed to the ever-gentle Una, was surprised into retreat before he remembered his dignity. After that, it was too late. The battle lines were drawn. We now lived in an armed camp so far as the dogs were concerned.

And then there were Charlie and Jasper, the cats.

Maggie's former owners, a man and his wife, had paid her a farewell visit at the school before we left, and had told me some of her background. She was raised without other pets around, so cats were going to be a novelty.

Charlie, the Siamese, observed her arrival from the back of the sofa, where he sat like a carving and eyed her with a stare that suggested pity for any creature so foolhardy as to annoy him. Maggie eyed him in turn, plainly puzzled as to what to make of him, and not at all sure she ought to investigate closer. At least, not right away.

Jasper, however, wasn't about to gamble on that. Before a friend brought him to us at the end of August, Jasper had been a half-grown stray living on potato peels in garbage dumps and learning about survival the hard way. One look at this big dog looming up in his kitchen and he knew what to do—leave.

Maggie knew what to do, too: chase him.

The race ended down the hall in my office. We found Jasper crouched on the bookshelf above my desk, Maggie jumping up and down in a tumble of books and tape cassettes on the floor. Maggie appeared to think Jasper was a marvelous toy, a huge improvement over an ordinary ball or even the tug-of-war toy she liked so well. She yipped at him to come down and play some more.

Poor Jasper. But it could have been worse. Sister, when I first brought her home, had lunged to kill the cats I had then. For months my family and I were on constant watch to keep her from doing them serious harm. She wouldn't be taught to tolerate them—until the day she leaped from an idling car in pursuit of a cat on the sidewalk.

That cat didn't run. He wrapped himself around her muzzle and hung on, front claws gouging her face, hind claws raking bloody fur-

Charlie and Jasper finally became friends with Maggie

rows under her jaw. She had been glad to get back in the car when he let her go, and she never showed an interest in any cat again.

Nevertheless, Maggie's wild enthusiasm could damage a small animal as severely as Sister's ill will.

"Maggie, no," I said sharply. "No kitty!"

It was a command which, within a week, became a refrain that Ted and I were repeating a dozen times a day.

And when it wasn't "No kitty," it was "No" something else. No, don't challenge Mike to a growling match. No, don't empty the wastebasket and shred the contents. No, leave Ted's slippers, my stockings, everybody's gloves alone. No, paws off the kitchen counter. No, don't ravel my knitting across the house. . . .

Letting Maggie loose in the house was like unleashing an indoor tornado.

One way to use up some of that energy was to take long walks. I began teaching her my favorite routes the day after we arrived home. To my delight, she found our driveway without prompting on only our second excursion up the road and back. She was also quick to grasp that we should walk on the side of the road, not down the center.

She was eager for each new adventure during those earliest weeks: meeting the neighborhood children, visiting friends, going shopping, dining out. We even attended a very loud concert where she astonished me by making no objection to the noise.

Then came the snow. It started Thanksgiving morning and kept on snowing for three days more. Bushes, rocks, mailboxes, small trees

vanished under drifts that rose even higher each time the snowplows pushed by.

Next, the thermometer dropped below zero and stuck there for over a week. It was too soon for winter to be clamping down in earnest, but clamped down it was.

On our first walk after the temperatures eased up some, Maggie stared around at the walls of snow on either side of the road as if we were on a different planet. We moved along at a brisk enough pace, though, until a little boy slid down a snowbank to greet us. Maggie had let him pet her a number of times on past walks, but this day she began to bark wildly at him and back away, twisting to hide herself behind me. There was no calming her, nothing to do but cut the walk short and turn back.

It was not a short walk, however. Maggie couldn't seem to find our driveway. We tramped up and down the road for half an hour while I pleaded, "Left and in," or, going the other direction, "Right and in," without success. At last we met a neighbor who guided us to the snow-

Long walks suited Maggie.

———

83

packed ruts we wanted, but at sight of her, Maggie went into the same barking, backing panic as before.

To say the least, it was a dismaying experience. Worse, it was one that was repeated with variations almost every time we went out. I learned to leave an electronic beeper chirping on the front porch to beam us home, but I never knew when someone approaching us on foot, a group of children playing in the snow, or a shopper in the next aisle was going to set Maggie off in another fit of hysterics.

Turning the house upside down with puppy mischief was one thing. That was to be expected. But falling apart because of a change of season—that made no sense whatever.

"Unless it's that people look sort of weird to her," a friend suggested, "everybody bundled up in snowmobile suits and parkas and ski masks and everything. Come to think of it, they look pretty weird to me, too."

That did make sense. Maggie's first winter, if she had any memory of it, was doubtless mild and short by Wisconsin standards, spent in the security of her Ohio backyard. Now, she was being asked to work in a suddenly white-on-white landscape where familiar landmarks, even smells, had been wiped out—one peopled by padded monsters with thick, oversized heads and arms that ended in leathery flippers and sometimes with no visible faces at all. There had been nothing to prepare her for this.

But what to do about it? I couldn't ask the monsters to peel in sub-zero weather to prove they were everyday humans. Neither was it any good using leash corrections when she panicked; they just made her more frantic.

"She's not much good as a guide dog this way," Ted said worriedly after New Year's. "Maybe you'll have to send her back."

Would I? The thought had crossed my mind, too.

"Maggie, Maggie, Maggie," I sighed, sitting down on the floor beside her. What shall I do with you?"

She jumped up and raced away from my hug. A moment later one of Ted's socks was thrust into my hand—clearly an item of value to me since I had made such a fuss when she carried them off.

"Maggie, Maggie," I said again, this time laughing.

She let go the sock and stamped her feet, an invitation for me to chase her.

It wasn't the solution to our problem, but it did answer my question. I wasn't about to part with her if I could help it. Not while there was any way in the world we might still work our way through this.

And we were far from having tried every possibility. Yet . . .

I GOT nowhere trying to convince Maggie that her monsters meant her no harm.

When the roadside children offered her treats I supplied from my pocket, she dodged from the outstretched mittens as if they were exploding firecrackers. She wouldn't touch the treats even when the children laid them in the snow and backed off to give her more space, although she was eager to claim the rescued tidbits from me when we got home.

Neither did she put any faith in a hand extended to her without a mitten or glove. Her tail might twitch faintly in recognition of a scent she'd known as a friend's before the snow, but the slightest move from the monster now attached to it, a nod or a smile, a shift of weight from one fleece-lined boot to the other and she was instantly on her guard, barking furiously at this attempt to trick her.

Oddly, we had no such problems on the streets in town. Maggie worked among dozens of winter-clad people as calmly as she ever did in Columbus.

The reason slowly dawned on me. These people paid her no special attention as they rushed to get their errands done and their chilled cars started. They simply went their way and let Maggie go hers.

So I stopped urging Maggie to let herself be petted by would-be friends. I asked people to ignore her as much as possible; not to speak to her, not to hold out a hand to her, not to look at her if they could avoid it.

And I stopped punishing her for being afraid. Instead, after a sharp "No" at the first signs of panic, I stooped down and hugged her, telling her she was a good girl after all, that she was safe, and that everything was going to be okay.

It took time. It took patience. It took helpful advice sent by Wayne Mathys, Director of Training at Pilot. But gradually, as the winter wore away, so did most of Maggie's fears.

She began to stand her ground at my side rather than bucking to hide behind me. She discovered she really could tell the difference between a dent in a snowbank and the opening to our driveway. She began to recognize the neighbors we met most often along the road and to give them a cautious wag instead of collapsing.

Most guide dog owners will agree it takes about six months for a dog and master to become a truly blended team. When it happens, it's like suddenly speaking the same language after months of trying to understand and be understood in a foreign tongue.

I'm afraid there were moments when I wondered if such communication were beyond the bounds of possibility for Maggie and me, but in early April the magic happened—right on schedule.

Perhaps the going of the snow had something to do with it. Within a matter of days the knee-high drifts and frozen ruts shrank away to nothing and we were walking at ease along bare roads smelling of spring and warm with sun.

Also, the thirtieth of March marked Maggie's second birthday. In terms of years, she was no longer a puppy.

That same week, Maggie and I went to visit my mother for several days. Since my mother's four cats do not enjoy being pounced on or chased by guests, Maggie stayed on leash at my side most of the time as she had during our training at Pilot Dogs. It was a refresher course in togetherness for both of us.

I realized we were working in a new way as we boarded our bus back to Rhinelander. The noise of three idling buses in the terminal swallowed spoken commands, but a motion of my hand or a touch on the leash were enough. Maggie understood what I wanted, and I was following her in complete confidence as she did it. We were beginning to think on the same wavelength.

Maggie knows the mailbox.

———

At the midway point of our journey we had to change buses. Moving with the other passengers into the waiting room and finding a seat was no problem at all.

Not everyone was as well pleased as I, however.

"A dog," shrilled a voice in front of me as if its owner had never seen such a thing before. "You can't bring a dog in here."

"This is a guide dog," I said. "She goes where I do. It's the law."

The woman ignored me. "I didn't know you let dogs in here," she told someone at the lunch counter in tones that penetrated to every corner. "It's supposed to be no dogs allowed."

I reached for the ID card in my purse. On one side of it is a picture of Maggie and me. On the other it states that she and I have successfully completed a course of training at Pilot Dogs, Inc., and are entitled to all the privileges granted guide dog owners by local, state, and federal law.

Along with this card I always carry a copy of the Wisconsin guide dog law, which reads:

"Wisconsin law guarantees a blind person the legal right to be accompanied by a specially

Gatekeeper at the Rhinelander Logging Museum learns from my ID card that the sign does not apply to Maggie.

trained dog guide in harness on all public accommodations. The dog guide user can be requested to submit for inspection the identification card provided by dog guide schools to their graduates. Public accommodations under Wisconsin law include hotels, inns, stores, restaurants, public conveyances on land and water, places of resort and recreation and all other facilities or places to which the general public is invited. Section 174.056.

"Violation: Any person or owner, lessee, employee or agent of a public accommodation who interferes with the above enumerated rights may be fined up to $100 or imprisoned for thirty days or both. Section 174.056."

Every state has a similar law as does Puerto Rico and each of the Provinces of Canada. Without these laws to protect a guide dog owner's right to go where sighted people do, the usefulness of a dog like Maggie would be severely limited. There are always persons who would keep dogs out of public places if they could, sometimes for no better reason than that they've never seen one there before.

Once a headwaiter refused to allow me into a wedding reception where I was an invited guest. The law didn't apply to a private party, he said. Luckily the father of the bride spotted us and set him straight.

Another time, a newly assigned campus guard would not let me enter the college building where I was an instructor in the English department—the same college from which I had graduated after four years of attending classes with my dog. The guard had decided on his own authority that dogs had no business in school, and nothing could persuade him otherwise until the college president arrived on the scene and personally escorted my dog and me inside.

Then there was the restaurant manager who insisted that because of my dog I could be served only outdoors on an open porch one sleety November day. "It's not that I don't like dogs," he wanted me to know, "but customers don't like them around where there's food. My own little dog at home never gets in our dining room, either. No, ma'am, we never let him anyplace in the house but the kitchen."

My guess was that the woman in the bus station had no liking for dogs wherever they might be.

A man at the lunch counter was loudly snuffling and coughing between unappetizing bouts of blowing his nose. Two little boys, apparently traveling alone, were scuffling near the door, swinging yoyos at each other and—accidentally, of course—at anyone else who happened in range. Yet the one thing in that room the woman chose to protest was Maggie, lying quietly at my feet, bothering nobody and in nobody's way.

Three different voices spoke up for Maggie—that of the bus driver, the girl behind the counter, and the older of the two boys. They all repeated what I had told the woman and remarked on what a beautiful, gentle, intelligent dog Maggie was.

I don't know if the woman boarded the same bus as Maggie and I when it came; I didn't hear her speak again.

I do know that Maggie responded to the admiring looks and voices of her champions by actually strutting out to the bus, head high, feet lifted daintily, tail in a jaunty curve. She was important, privileged, altogether special, and she knew it.

I hugged her as we settled ourselves for the long journey still ahead. Because I knew it, too.

———